How I Got Lost
So Close to Home

Amy Dryansky

For Jeannine —
Fellow tent-dweller!
Best, Amy

ALICE JAMES BOOKS
Farmington, Maine

Book design by Gillian Drake

COVER ARTWORK: *Goddess Nut,* 1989 (detail) by Nancy Spero,
photographed by David Reynolds. Photo courtesy of P.P.O.W.
and Jack Tilton Gallery, New York.

AUTHOR PHOTO: Robin Todd

Epigraph from "On the Road Home" from *Collected Poems* by
Wallace Stevens. Copyright 1954 by Wallace Stevens. Reprinted
by permission of Alfred A. Knopf Inc.

LIBRARY OF CONGRESS CATALOGING-PUBLICATION DATA

Dryansky, Amy, 1960-
  How I got lost so close to home / Amy Dryansky.
    p. cm.
  ISBN: 1-882295-22-6 (paper)
  1. Women - - Poetry. I. Title.
PS3554.R865 H69 1999
811'.54—dc21
                                          99-11029
                                            CIP

Printed in the United States of America

FIRST EDITION

9 8 7 6 5 4 3 2 1

Alice James Books gratefully acknowledges support
from the University of Maine at Farmington and the
National Endowment for the Arts.

Alice James Books are published by the
ALICE JAMES POETRY COOPERATIVE, INC.
University of Maine at Farmington
98 Main Street
Farmington, Maine 04938

This book is for John

In memory of my father
9-3-27 — 8-25-99

Acknowledgments

My thanks to the editors of the following periodicals, in which a number of the poems in this book first appeared (some in earlier versions) or are forthcoming:

Bloomsbury Review: "Too Small to Keep"
DoubleTake: "Creative"
the eleventh MUSE: "What the Tin Man Didn't Know"
Green Mountains Review: "Black Crumbs," "Out of Here"
Harvard Review: "Merit Badge"
The Louisville Review: "The Size of a Bed Sheet" (published as "South America")
Luna: "Bedtime," "Black Pouches"
The Marlboro Review: "How It Flew from Her"
The Massachusetts Review: "The Lull Between Spokes"
Mudfish: "The Intersection of Yes"
New England Review: "Aboard"
Peregrine: "Solitary Vireo"
Southern Poetry Review: "Amber"
Work: "Northern Garden"

"A Short Message" also appeared in the *Anthology of New England Writers* (Seventh Annual Free Verse Contest Issue, 1995)

I am grateful to the MacDowell Colony and Vermont Studio Center for their amazing gift of residencies during which I was able to work on this book; the Ludwig Vogelstein Foundation for a grant which enabled me to take advantage of a residency; and to the Bread Loaf Writers Conference, where I broke my promise never to wait tables again.

This book wouldn't have happened without the faith and support of my teachers, friends and family. Particular thanks to: my faculty advisors at Vermont College; the Alice James Books collective, especially Janet Kaplan, Ellen Watson and Peg Peoples; past and present members of the Po Group, Word Girls and my Wednesday night workshop; cherished friends and insightful critics Carlen Arnett and Robyn Oughton; my daughter Madeleine, for showing me what's possible; and my parents, who already believed I could do anything.

Contents

I

II

It was when I said,

"There is no such thing as the truth,"

That the grapes seemed fatter,

The fox ran out of his hole.

—Wallace Stevens, "On the Road Home"

I

Today Everything Hurts

Especially the man holding open the Rent-A-Center door
for his wife, and her white vinyl purse.
The shining hair of the clerk who will greet them.
The woman in a souvenir sweatshirt wheeling
an empty cart.
The baby seat in the back of the van.
The man in the green compact driving his mother.
How they both look straight ahead.
The pink display of little girls' bikes
tipped precisely on their kickstands
like a line of Rockettes.
The Rockettes would hurt, too, if they were here.
Like that woman's feet must hurt
standing outside the drug store with a cigarette
waiting who knows how long for her ride
in those cheap shoes.
The music piped-in to the parking lot.
The woman trying not to shake the screaming child.
The child's older sister trying to keep out of the way.
It looks like she can't.

Merit Badge

Mine's a stone-gray, scrap-metal rosette
spiked with three-penny nails and a Howdy-Doody smile.
It says *Most Improved, Congeniality, Goes Down
With the Ship.* Says if you hurt me, I'll laugh. If you hurt me
harder, I'll laugh harder. It says better
to curl into a tight ball beneath the kitchen table
than say *Will you look at me, really look at me?*
Will you put down your vacuum cleaner attachments,
and your laundry basket and cheap scotch-on-the-rocks,
your Walter Cronkite and pseudo-left politics and your parties
where everybody sings *If I Had A Hammer* way into the night
    and in the morning
I cruise through the leftover chips and dips and overturned
    ashtrays and glasses
rimmed with red wine or lipstick or my father's famous punch;
cruise through and survey, knowing today
even my mother gets up late. My merit badge is to let them sleep.
It says *Her A's are predictable, she seems to be popular, she's always
out with her friends.* My merit badge sits on my chest
like a leather button on an old army coat. It says *Do not remove
under penalty of law.* It says don't tell, don't tell
if you break something or something breaks you. Don't ask.
Keep your teeth clean. Make it look like an accident. My badge says
she's lost but won't tell you why, found but doesn't know it.
The badge says push here and here and here and breathe. Back up,
try it again. Here and here and here and breathe. Close your eyes.
This time it works. A goldfinch like a piece of the sun flies down
and steals what she thinks is a black seed from my badge.
And I let her. My merit badge says I let her.

14

Too Small to Keep

Lately I've wanted to kiss my husband
as if he were a handsome stranger,
which he is, when his face clouds up

and I hear the distant thunder
of a foot stomp.
I'd like to kiss that foot, with joy,

with total inattention.
I'd like to amputate my own wooden anger,
clear my lap of its dumb ventriloquist's doll

and invite my handsome stranger to sit.
We'd eat an enormous breakfast,
unplug our appliances,

pull the shades and pretend
no one lives here, has ever lived here,
with an opinion or social security number.

She's been replaced by a flamenco dancer,
he by her lover, Thor, and they are very busy
eating breakfast with no clothes on,

and they are not cold
in their nakedness, not ashamed, they love
all the places on each other

others do not, especially the overabundance
of loam, backwash, riprap.
They believe in the rain.

They've set up camp with nothing
but breakfast and black sheets
and a wind-up alarm clock set at midnight.

At midnight they can see in the dark.
At midnight he hides his spurs in the sweet hay.
At midnight she finally stops grooming.

At midnight they remember everything
they forgot about each other,
forget everything they knew;

she throws an invisible net in the air,
he makes himself a silver-bellied fish,
they take turns catching

and getting caught, throwing back,
easing the barbed hook from their mouths.
At midnight they eat, and the clock

keeps not striking twelve.

Creative

I was listening to *On Broadway*,
and George Benson gets to the part about time
and how he wants to make some,

except he's broke so he can't,
and I start thinking about what that means.
He's talking about the kind of time

people make when they're into each other,
like Jamie Moody and me in my parents' den;
neither of us had any money—I was in junior high

and Jamie delivered school lunches out of a van—
but that didn't keep us from making time.
Except a lot of people might say

women don't make time, but represent
what it's made from: the punch line, the putty, the proof—
or even the black hole, that mystery

where gravity stands on its head.
And Jamie was Black. So though a man, maybe
not as powerful as he deserved.

But even if it was never enough, Jamie and I together
definitely made something.
He couldn't have done it without me,

and I always felt like I got my share.
Which is why, after my mother's third knock on the wall,
her signal we had—finally, really—to say goodnight,

there was always that shock we could
separate. We thought the world changed with us.
Instead, we woke to the same itchy tweed couch

and unwatched TV, our warm digits folded into laps,
and mouths gone back to their second-best purpose:
making promises, songs about what's lost.

The Intersection of Yes

I chose him. Put myself in his path like a dropped tree limb.
Uneager to dance, he was unlike the tenth-grade boys,

and only walked me home because his friend wanted mine.
While they kissed we stared at one another, and he finally

got the point. I can't remember how we came together,
just the smell of his jacket collar, and how warm with his neck

the navy fake fur was: an indigo cloud, a blue Persian wound
around itself. After that we kissed every chance we got,

one wall or another pressed into my spine, his arms
describing my body like expertly thrown knives.

Maybe I felt like that, his assistant. Trusted him,
or wanted to die. Because we talked so little

I used to wonder what he thought
of me, and when I finally got the nerve to ask

it was a stupid question: if kissing me was different
than kissing a Black girl. He laughed.

I don't know what I meant, except now I think
I feared him missing something: an essential salt

I lacked or the inside of my mouth emptier than it should be.
Sometimes I couldn't tell his tongue from mine.

But the question didn't melt down, it became a stone
that set itself. Between us, light began to show:

pleasure no longer simply what we breathed
into each other, but measured by how much and how far.

Now, his friend said, he knew a girl who *gave it up,*
and the lack I suspicioned, the missing part was named,

and it undid me. Took away sweetness, made me think
of columns thick with numbers. Didn't I want to

keep him? Yes. I agreed to the trade, set some conditions,
delayed, negotiated and eventually

changed my mind. Even now I'm not sure if we
crossed a line or drew it, just that afterwards I missed him.

What the Tin Man Didn't Know

I do not understand the heart, how its chambers
divide, which of those built-up veins goes in

and which out, or how it works—if it's true
that removed from the body it could beat

for a moment or two in a cold metal tray,
or if that's just something I saw in a movie.

I don't know why it beats to begin with,
but tend to think it's an accident, that the heart

is well placed, adequately formed, and amenable
to dull, hard work. It's stout. Other muscles

tighten to a cramp and stay there,
joints protest they are always under fire,

overworked, fed up with the union,
and the blood, too, is hard to count on: in winter

humping along like thick soup, then in spring,
thoughtless—a salty freshet pushing headlong

through the veins, rising in the nape to pool
in the muddy low spots of the brain.

Why the heart? Why the idealized
shape, cherubim, doilies, bluebirds and arrows

piercing without a drop of blood? And why,
when the object of desire is won, do two

hearts press against breastbone and rib, earnestly
trying to turn their breathing from passionate

counterpoint to dumb beats in time? As if love
never happened before, were never going to again.

How I Got Lost So Close to Home

Fear pushes me into the rowboat and tells me to row.
The oars are worn, bruised by the locks, poor handling, repetition,
   salt.
Meanwhile, my mother rolls out the crust for another apple pie,
pushing down on the widening circle. She's figured out
how to keep the dough from tearing, and I will learn this

from her, as with everything else, through observation.
She's too busy for lessons. And I lose something in translation,
or distance. Is fear rolling pin or dough? Force or substance?
What transforms the room at night? What snuffs the lamps?
Fear says I do. We argue, but I keep rowing. I am in love with fear

and fear knows it. I want to climb into fear's lap, unbutton his shirt,
put my face against his chest. I know it's warm there. Fear knows
I don't mean this, brays, shows his yellow teeth to remind me
he's an ass. *You expected Cary Grant, maybe?* my mother asks,
shakes her head, wipes her hands on a dish towel.

I open the oven door and check the pie so she can't see
how the light has gone out of my face. Wasn't it she
who introduced us? How could I imagine she'd want anything less
for me, anything other than the best? Fear smiles,
Now you're talking, he says, *now we're cooking with gas.*

A Short Message

She said toward the end all she could
feel was tired, all she wanted
was to stop moving.

We were supposed to have dinner.
I let her phone ring the polite eight times.
When no one answers, you wonder
what they're doing, if they're having fun.

When I called again the machine was on,
and I thought maybe
she wasn't really out, maybe
she'd decided to blow me off.

I could hear you on the line,
chewing, she said, *imagine you*
eating all of that food, our meal, yourself.
He thought it was funny
when you called me that name.

When I called he'd been raping her
for six hours.
I'd left a message to tell her
what I ordered: Szechuan chicken,
hot-and-sour soup, two spring rolls.
You're an asshole, I'd said,
You don't know what you're missing.

Out of Here

Most people embrace dawn's unblinking,
catholic illumination, but I'd rather disappear
behind drawn shades. Bright mornings

leave me shaken, transparent—like a player at bat
who's lost her nerve, I knock a lot
of imaginary dirt from my shoes,

and though I'm pretty good at stepping away
from a circle before it's drawn,
even I get distracted. Light is seductive,

easy—like everyone else I start to like it
that my back is warm, and I forget,
turn my profile to its best advantage

when I know darkness is safer. Better
invisible than pitied, I say,
and if I'm going to be disappointed

I want to see it coming. The way it was
clear by the sixth inning at last week's game
that the Sox were going to lose again. But even before

the crowd booed Clemens off the mound,
I was out of the game, watching
the guy in front of me get drunk. Honking

like a goose at every call, he told us all
what he thought of who and why.
I wanted to tell him to pull up his pants.

By that time I'd missed two double plays,
our team's only run, and I couldn't say when exactly
they took Clemens out,

but I'd remembered my binoculars,
and from my last row seat beneath the overhang
I could see the expression on his face

as Clemens walked off, something
the fans screaming from the hot bleachers
wouldn't bother with, nor the season ticket holders,

who are so used to being close they're numb.
And the girl up front who got knocked out by a foul,
you wouldn't believe the way the crowd

cheered when they carried her out.
As if she'd seen it coming, as if it took guts
to get yourself socked in the eye.

The Lull Between Spokes

There's a girl in me with blue knee-socks
and a caved-in wingspan.
She's got her mother's heart that does not rest,
her grandfather's hunger, her father's
rage. God knows what else.
She has to work hard to find unusually bright flowers,
thinks she could die if she stops,
if she's not brim full with sweet stuff. She's listening

to my father's furious voice
spiral up the stairwell, she can almost see his anger
lift my mother off her feet.
But she's never not afraid long enough to look.
Chair? Ashtray? Hand?
For God's sake, or *don't,* my mother says, then the pause—
He's done, the girl tells herself,
and hides the knife stolen from the silverware drawer.

That lull is what I most recall,
like it or not;
my chest vibrating as if a brood of doves
crowded there. They make a regular murmur,
a safe and stupid noise,
until I think I hear a lady's ivory fan snap shut
against her palm, or else
so hard a slap her head jerks back,
and the doves fly out.

I'm always hearing things.
When as a kid my legs ached I thought
my bones were trying to talk— .
my mother said they were just growing—and I imagined
I could hear them knitting,

the way she did at the movies,
a brittle, white song of needles in the dark.

It made me curious. Full-length
naked, I'd stare into the bathroom mirror,
and taking up the slack skin around my elbows and knees,
pull. As if I could draw out
what was hidden there—a kind of failure,
black-spotted, fast as cancer—before it could catch me
by surprise.

Sometimes I caught a glimpse of it. Once,
when I was five
and my grandfather made me drop my towel
on the way to the shower.
Pointing at me from his plastic-sheathed, crushed
velvet recliner, he gestured
at my two hands holding the ends of the towel together
like he was telling one of his stock boys
where to stack a case of peaches.

Show me what you got under there, what have you got?
My mother said, *Go ahead.*
She's modest, she told him, but it wasn't that.
I didn't understand what,
but only let him see for the barest of seconds, and still,
it felt like he left something
there. On my body. Or had he seen what I suspected
was already in place?

The girl in me is disappearing into a pillar—
alert for the train's low roar,
the rush of pneumatic doors letting go—she's always

got a better place to be.
But trying to leave she looks back, because
I've got a cynic in there, too,
and he loves her. Even the crooked bones
in the pinkie that never healed right.
Or because.

Because it wasn't doves,
it was pigeons under the eaves, their chatter
every morning that woke me, their shit
spattering my windows, pigeons
repeating the same words over and over,
and she's always waiting
for the doves, or him, or somebody like him
she's trying to love, to start again.

Amber

Inside the sugar maples' locked branches
something clear has begun
to come loose; it will be caught, held,

plied with intense heat.
I pity the pink tips of those branches,
their forced march in the dark

before the clocks catch up.
And I pity myself, swaddled bones
scraping food from the same black pot.

I hear the maples, their drip.
I watch the sky above the sap house
darken with ash, light up

with sparks as the boiling continues
into the night and the crude
outlines of the bright windows beckon.

I zip my high-necked dress up the back,
its straight silver teeth obediently close;
I'm so cold it feels like music.

Solitary Vireo

I understand why people drive around
with their stereos up and their windows down;
sometimes it's not enough to burn alone
inside, you want everyone, the world,

to feel your heat, char their fingers
picking you out of the crowd.
But the guy who sells you a scratch ticket
drops your change on the counter

right next to your upturned palm,
and the clerk in the booth at the bank,
and the gas station, and the fast-food drive-thru,
shuts off her intercom before you can

tell her what you want—
maybe you'll steal from her.
Maybe you take your white-hot ache,
turn it inside out, wave it, snap it

open like a toreador's cape. Maybe for a while
you feel like a bullfighter—
except the bull won't charge. So you go
to the park because you always go,

and while you're there some old lady
grabs your arm and points:
Vireo, she says, *vireo.*
Jesus, you think, but you're tired,

so take her binoculars and look, see
the startled round eye of a bird,
its chest pushing out notes.
You're still looking

while the woman reads to you from her book:
A common migrant in most of the East.
Loud song of short, varied phrases repeat
See-me, hear-me, here-I-am.

For Your Excellent Service

Thanks for filling my tank.
Thanks for smiling.
Thanks for hearing the exact words I said.
Thanks for responding.
Thanks for making a joke that was not at my expense.
Thanks for making it with me.
Thanks for looking at me close up,
        for seeing all the way through to the elemental
        lining of my dark gray cloud.
Thanks for wanting it to rain.
Thanks for praying to get soaked.
Thanks for not covering up, not taking shelter, not watching
        from a safe, dry spot.
Thanks for getting wet with me.
Thanks for drying me off, for pulling the rubber squeegee
        across my windshield at just the right angle
        and shaking off the dross.
Thanks for wiping the length of the soft blade
        with a dry chamois cloth,
        then convincing me to slide my hand down
        under the dash to release the latch,
        so you could check my oil.
Thanks for finding the spot where the slender rod props the hood
        without my having to show you.
Thanks for showing me the space between the optimum fill line
        and where my oil glistened,
        and recommending I put in a quart or two,
        just to be sure.
Thanks for writing it all up on a tissue-y carbon for me
        to autograph,
        tearing off my copy, keeping one for yourself,
        and holding the pen I'd just held in my hand
        in your mouth, as I drove away.

Northern Garden

No one embraces a lack, but some are satisfied
with little, they celebrate

finding a politician's face in a potato—
while the more ambitious crave holiness

in the ordinary: the Virgin's face in tree bark,
Devil in a craggy stone peak,

anything you can dream up
in a cloud. Me, I keep telling this story

about flowers, these three boxes of pansies
I planted, each a different shade—

yellow-eyed maroon, purple and blue
with butter-white throats—

but as the weeks passed, and the plants took root
in their plot, they began to change,

seemed to choose their best expression
until they all looked like

blue ribbons back from the fair, the same
face upturned, prize-winning, smug student.

To me it's science fiction—or lately,
just science—like how doctors are learning

to change muscle into bone, they say
you have to want to get well—

rats do it, so we can't be far behind—
but what did those pansies want?

I imagine their desire
is no different than ours: to belong,

be safe, become part of an unbroken line
in which the void of one past bloom

can go unnoticed.
Maybe I'm making a big deal

out of nothing—the change came so slowly—
maybe it didn't happen at all,

but when friends drop by,
we walk out to the garden's unruly beds

and I offer them my story, as if flowers
alone are never enough.

Few Minutes

The white lilies at intervals
like music, reaching up.
Scent, where the wind takes it,
each to each.
The summersweet nodding its gooseneck
boughs this way and that,
white in the shade.
I'm not ready.
I'm not ready to come in.
I haven't said any, or enough.

Black Crumbs

for my father

What has its thick finger in my throat
must be like the balloon the cardiologist used
to unblock my father's arteries, their narrow halls
papered a yellowing white with what my father
for years ingested: sweetbreads, *kishke, gribinev,*
tripe, the slippery dark meat that clings to neck bones
you eat with your fingers, your whole open mouth.
He, in turn, must feel against his chest
his father, pressing a loaf of dark rye to his work shirt,
cutting a good, thick slice of heel he hands
to my father, who can't swallow for watching
the knife saw toward my grandfather's heart, the black crumbs
falling. The balloons were supposed to clear all that
poor man's food, that yeasted promise,
from my father's future. But he loves beauty and perhaps
can't help loving that he, too, could live
close to the knife and then succumb like his father, abruptly
disappearing into death before the house
they're building together is complete. Too modest for a dream,
but sturdy, and if the windows seem small, the ceilings
low and dark, *it could be worse,* he says
to my father, thinking of his father, my great-grandfather.
It could be bread soaked in beer and baked for hardtack,
a coat sewn with cloth-covered rubles for buttons,
a middle-of-the-night exit, a house too poor for a clock
to mark the minutes left, and a girl fallen asleep in the kitchen
waiting to say good-bye to her brother—
is she the sister who died going over the fence at Auschwitz,
or the sister who survived? It doesn't matter.
He doesn't wake her before he goes, they don't see each other
again. In America he has his story to tell,
and the story about his father, who traded horses
to the Cossacks, first filing down the black spots

on their teeth, so they'd look prime.
A horse that's not strong, can't be ridden, won't haul—
is it better to have that horse
than nothing? And my grandfather's father—
a Jew, the Cossacks he sold his nags to,
is there something about transactions, a willingness
to deceive and be deceived, that blesses us all?

II

The Size of a Bed Sheet

A woman sits back on her heels.
Alone by a deep, green river,
she washes a brightly colored cloth
the size of a bed sheet.
It tugs at her hands, twists downstream
but she holds on, winding it in
to rub against the rocks, releasing it
to unfurl beneath the water.
The woman is lost in the rhythm of her work
and remembering the life of the cloth.
She ticks off on imaginary fingers
the special occasions of its use:
when she had to pack all she owned in an hour
and move deeper into the hills.
As a tent when she had no other shelter.
To make one room into two when her children got older.
As a shroud for her husband.
As a shroud for her son.
She thinks again how lucky she was to get it,
how rare: a piece so big without any holes.

Reticular

Inside the dryer's metal drum
shoulder grazes shoulder
on white undershirts, socks
pair, roll, disappear.

I stare at the seams in my hands,
the honeycomb of the cool tile floor,
every one of six sides
joined to another just like—even
the holes in the washer's empty basket
come equally spaced, and there are so many.

I open my palms again, lean into them.
I think they can tell me something
I want my whole body to hear:
the seams, emptiness, supplication.

I don't believe in you.
I've never believed in you.
I want you to save me anyway.

Undone

Think of Joan before she was a saint.
When she fears her voices
have abandoned her and she recants,
will take everything back,
even *put off her man's dress,*
not to feel her body burn. Without grace
she, like everyone else
can't bear to see what comes next:

> if someone saves you,
> if you save yourself,
> if the bottom exists,
> if that stops you,
> if another bottom
> lies beneath the one you just hit.

I'm thinking of another story.
In our bedrooms radiating out from the hall
I am one petal, and around me
my brothers, sisters and parents, too,
are petals on the same stalk. Asleep.
Who is it then who wakes me—
hand over my face—
to a seasick, irregular rocking?

> When the bough breaks,
> when the office tower floors give way
> and the elevator, your breath
> plummets in its vault, do you
> uncurl your fingers from your bed's
> narrow plank
> and stay, follow the dream down?

I'm very young. I don't discriminate.
I know it hurts but I don't know
it isn't supposed to happen.
Like Joan, I have my instructions—
mine not to ride forth but to lie still,
and these not from a beatific Catherine or Margaret
but someone become someone else
in the dark. I tell myself
maybe it's just another kind of plate-cleaning
the dessert comes after,

       but in the morning I'm just alone
       with a kind of blindness. No one sees
       how I've changed, how I'm still in the air.

Rash Refrain

I can't decide if the two red streaks
on either side of my mouth
are commas or question marks:
is there more, or are we done asking?

No one but me and my sister
can see the red. No one
but me can feel it. My sister is sorry:
she'd like to know more, but won't ask me.

The streaks are hot and they burn,
especially when I drink the good reds:
Beaujolais, Bordeaux, Burgundy.
I could give them up, but no one's asked me.

One doctor says here's some cream.
One doctor says cream just pushes it down.
I'm supposed to let it rise and redden and peel.
After all, there's always fresh skin
underneath: more skin, more asking?

Black Pouches

Holding in silence with a two-fisted yank
and a fine Celt knot (no visible start or end,
nothing to work back and undo),
the black pouches gleam. I sit with some in my lap,

stroke their velvet as if they were kittens,
and one opens the way a snake's jaw
relaxes around a meal twice its size.
If I stick my head inside I can see

last night's undigested dream: a younger me
unearthing treasure from beneath my bedroom floor.
Shiny crow bait. Incongruous food.
(I'm looking for joy.) I finger the pouches

like a miser his gold. It's good to be good
at something, and I'm so good at stuffing
these pouches my brothers dubbed me
with the only nickname I've known: *Packrat.*

The pouches grow ears, legs, long naked tails,
begin to scrabble over each other, sniffing,
and I picture my dark mouse self
dragging discards back to my room,

sorting through, fixing, bundling, binding, settling
on some irrational, felt, talismanic arrangement.
It's true. I stole. But only what I thought
no one else would want or miss.

Rifling each cupboard and closet and high shelf,
I'd search for something I'd recognize
when found, or it found me (joy!):
shirt cardboard, scrap fabric, lidless boxes,

discards my family noticed
only after I'd got my hands on them,
when I was almost done
making them look like something you'd want.

The pouches nod their heads;
to this point there's been only unreachable fruit,
a vine adapting itself to a nearby support,
a nest of discomforting weave,

but now all the pouches open—as if the joy were there,
in making and remaking
that dark child, that dark house.
I go through them again, this time with a flashlight

that works, two matching socks,
and a warm winter coat;
I take my father's six-foot retractable measure,
my mother's soft lingerie,

my sister's homemade wedding dress,
and every window, thermos, pair of glasses
my little brother broke;
I bring the policeman who found me lost,

his gun, his radio, his confidence, his shock
no one knew I was missing;
I pack a calculator for my wasted education,
string of boyfriends, unborn babies,

friends who tried to help; I make sure
I've got at least one headache,
one thumb on the scale, one letter
with postage due. I've got these pouches,

a needle, a spool of tough, black thread,
yards more velvet.

Aboard

They say home's where the heart is, but what if it's only a place
to put your stuff? Like the toothbrush you chose
for its extra-hard bristle, but also because in the morning
you like to see the purple stem in your cup. Or those flowery
soaps you buy to make a shower more than sloughing off
debris from another ordinary day. Or maybe the day wasn't
so ordinary, you didn't just push the wheelbarrow:
empty-full, full-empty. You had one of those moments
you know you're alive,
or older than you thought you'd ever get,
or living with somebody you're not sure you love.
But maybe you've had enough of introspection.
You're afraid you spend too much time alone,
not just alone-alone, but alone-in-the-world, and you're not
bumping up against enough people, people that might
scare you, or you wouldn't want to have dinner with them,
or maybe you would, maybe you'd like to
snatch the food right off their plates.
You're thinking it's a long time since you rode the subway.
Does something begin to rust shut? Soften? Maybe it's too late.
Like everyone else you stood outside night after night
to catch sight of the comet. You learned to see the tail
without looking right at it. You almost got bored
until you remembered how important it was. Sort of
like the first time you saw a taco: seventh grade, Levy Junior High,
Clare Ehling has two on her lunch tray. You ask
what they are and she acts like you've been living in a shoe.
Maybe she's right. You can't even find time to paint the bathroom,
what about Tuscany, Bach, fame, childbirth?
Maybe home's an oversized tackle box
bursting with what you can't give away: a myth
of bliss and slow-running sap. You've swallowed it all.
You should've got while the getting was good.

Your ankle's developing an anchor
a whole lot faster than your eye's cultivating
a rakish black patch. That parrot on your epaulette
you've been parading—it's probably a crow.
Which explains why no one understands her. It makes you
wonder: how many leaks can one boat spring?

Dog on Hind Legs

Every night the dog down the road
asks the same question in an afflicted howling
I don't understand. But I picture her
tarpapered house with its upside-down U,
her metal stake sunk into a patch of cement,
and the rusted chain's rattle—which I do
understand—as she paces its length
in the packed-dirt circle she's worn in the ground.
When she barks I listen—
because she's found something to protect
in this neighborhood. I see only silhouettes
of what no longer exists: every dependable stick,
every dream with marrow gone.

Interval

It's not the random act you fear, but the known,
or what you thought you knew—its accumulation
on the path you're walking, the lichen-covered stones,
green above, silver below; the logical sequence
of pine descending to aspen and beech, their pale understory
leaves massed face down, ribs in sharp relief
—and none of it your business, you're the stranger, the only one
thinking, and how poor a job that's become
just now, when what you need is to feel, or start
to feel, how empty makes a different ache than full;
when what you need is to tell, or start
to tell, how it is the world's beauty could hurt you.

Bedtime

Because when I was drunk anything seemed possible,
and I wanted to feel something, other than alone,
I did it with men I barely knew (in doorways,
standing up, with a bad cough,
whatever). Not like in the movies—no panoramic
flowering of shattered china
swept from the dinner table's twisted white linen,
then the ceiling shot—the couple
frenzied, intent, smoking.
Our urgency was polite. We turned our heads
while digging into each other, trying to take everything
with us, as if fucking were magic, a fairy tale
in which an entire town, your life (the bookstore job,
A's in philosophy, days spent playing pool),
could get small enough to stuff into a drawstring pouch.
I found a spot on the wall to stare at.
I don't know what they did.
But I'd leave before the light outlining the window shade
could show us up: my soft hips, him
trying to figure out if he'd have to give me breakfast.
(It reminded me of how in spring the snow draws back
from junk that's been there all along.)
I'd go home through the park, to prove
I was charmed, could pass through violence
the way I had indifference.
Walking home, my disappointment felt like a curiosity—
something I might find on the ground, a relic
of bone-like white plastic split off from something larger.
It felt important so I'd keep it, try to imagine
what that something was.

Beauty Locked Up

It's like satisfaction follows a rule
I'm always bending.
Tonight we needed to open
one present after another,
and all I could do was box and unbox
the same cheap prize.
I kept my face lit.

But when we played a game
in which we had to admit the most debased state
we could imagine ourselves in,
what came to me was the hot-dog whistle
hidden in specially marked packages
of Oscar Mayer franks.

I begged my mother to buy them, even though
we always ate the kosher kind. *Please.*
Just this once. And she did. Of course,
there was nothing—just lousy hot dogs, but I
acted as if they were good.

These minor disappointments, I'm afraid
are just that, and the animal we heard
through the strains of the Birthday Song—
circling the barn, tracking food,
or in pain, or wanting to mate—
I'd rather hook-and-eye the door, I don't want to
know what it wants.
Just this once. Please.

Better look at the moon.
Even when there's less of her, she's got beauty
all locked up. Which might explain
that animal's raw complaint—
between you and me, I think it's why
I tend to eat too much,
make a show of clearing away the cake,
when I'm really back at it.

My "sweet tooth."
It's embarrassing, dark,
even a little comical, like getting caught
in my first conscious lie: the wriggling
runt kitten I tried to hide
from my grandfather's ether-soaked rag.
I was in love, not with the kitten,
but the secret pressed beneath my shirt,
the possibility I could make
a different kind of beauty.

Beneath the Canopy of Trees

for my mother

I don't know if my mother was ever a real dancer,
but she taught dance classes; I was one of her students.

At the beginning of class we girls in our pale pink leotards
sat in a circle and imagined dipping our toes into water.

We'd arch each foot until we felt the muscles
all the way up our legs contract, then quick

curl our toes back and shriek, *Ooh, it's cold!*
Then we'd line up behind my mother with our new-found tiptoes

dotting the basement linoleum, and leap away
from the icy pool she'd had us dip them in.

Whither shall I follow, follow, follow thee?
The song we danced to was called *The Greenwood,*

and it made me feel we were underwater, submerged
but buoyant, with fathom-high trees

waving like seaweed above our heads.
My mother and I don't talk about those days,

not even when she wakes at night and needs someone
to sit her up—she doesn't have a bell to ring,

just says my name, or sometimes, *help*. Her body is heavy
in my arms, like unseasoned wood, and it's hard

to be gentle because I'm not that strong.
When her body isn't stiff it shakes: jaw, arms, hands

keeping time, each with a slightly different rhythm.
Maybe her body can't decide,

maybe part of her is still in the Greenwood. I wouldn't blame her
for wanting to go back—it's like when I forgot

my part in our recital, and was so ashamed I ran off the stage
and hid. My father said it was O.K., *we can't all be stars,*

but I think the bright lights and the sets
confused me; I wish they'd given me another chance.

My mother wants me to sit with her until she falls asleep.
The magazine she was trying to read

slides off the bed, and it seems too late, almost cruel,
to tell my mother how much I loved her

when she led us through that dark, underwater forest.
I would have followed her into anything.

Beauty in Spite of, Not Because

Everyone is quick to say
I'm prettier than I look. From up high:

that's how I'd like to see myself,
like the time I climbed Monadnock, and saw

yellow-gold clouds below me
I thought were wildflowers moving in the wind,

but they were tree tops. Still, I like to
write about the hummingbird's pulsing iridescence

as it drinks from a stand of purple phlox—
as if by describing it I include myself.

So the bird I'm writing is a particular bird.
It fed at my mother's garden

beside the screened-in porch, and it's there,
with the speed of that ruby-throat's wings,

that I must hold,
because if I look up I see behind the screen

my mother—who I'd rather remember at Far Rockaway,
younger than I am now, but with the same squinting distrust

of the camera—but something about the way she stands
motionless on the dark porch—split into shadow

by the overhang—reminds me instead of a crowded London square
where for no good reason, a woman punched my mother

hard in the stomach. There was nothing beautiful
about my mother's stopped face, or my father's back

receding into the crowd, or me—not wanting to lose either of them—
finally urging my mother on. And now,

amidst all the kiosks, sausage-roll vendors, souvenir hawkers
pushing carts of miniature landmarks—

I've lost the bird completely.
That square wasn't beautiful, and I was brown—hair, eyes,

deep corduroy furrows, and crepe-soled shoes
with laces coming undone. There was never any time

to rest. I promised I would always make my bed, but I didn't
and that was that, my Mom said, no more promises. No beauty

here, either, not even the symbolic glow of poverty—we weren't poor,
and despite scab, and no one pruning space between their limbs—

our apple trees bore. But this, too, is not quite
beautiful. Even if I stand outside the dining room window,

it's varnished, amber-caught, a bad photograph. I'd rather
remember Monadnock: near the summit it was cold—

my legs and fingers were cramping—if I fell it would not be
into soft arms. The impact would strip my clothing from me—

even my shoes—leave my torn frame unrecognizable, hard to look at
up close, but from above easily passed over or mistaken

for something else—level ground, a picnic site,
a welcome, flesh-colored break in the yellow.

Unsought Prize

At this hour what is living should be dead,
and I, for now, am neither:
high in a closed cell of a room,
two slits from waist to head
for windows, a single, grim tapestry
concealing the bolted door.

Since there is nothing else
I study the tapestry—my sisters' patient work—
and instantly regret it;
the scene portrays a ride to hunt—a fox
surrounded by too many nobles, curs
masquerading as courtiers,

and I feel the rough, jute sack slip over
my head, the bump, bump,
of my back against the horse's flank
with its rank, domesticated stink.

At the castle they'll release me
in the keep, for sport,
to poke at me with sticks
while I run frantic circles. I will not
disappoint them. '
I'll bare my teeth and whine,
I'll give up,
exhausted, and when they close in
won't bother to lift my head
from the cool, stone floor.

What a trial for a thief to bear
a tail such as mine!—this banderole
of leaves and dry hay ignited,

this obvious, useless beauty
growing out of my ass.
I'm not much for introspection—and caught as I am
in this barking, slobbering noose
it's hard to imagine anything
but death—

but if I were to consider its nature
I'd say beauty, to me, lies
in planning. Finding what works
and sticking to it.
I'm not the fastest hunter in these woods,
my eyes not hawk-bright, I can't
freeze like the stag—or even the mouse—
who disappear by holding their breath.
But I have some tricks—
they say I'm sly, but I call it stealth,
and practice it well enough
to satisfy my hunger—

and if not for this tail, this unsought prize,
I might be closeted in my own sweet den,
warmed by the small bones of less adept peers,
instead of here, where my skills
count for nothing, and I am beset
by those who, even now, crave
the next entertainment.

The Space on the Floor Where the Dog Lay

feels warm to my bare feet,
and I think I see a dark outline
his body's left, and picture crossing
through shadows, following him
from one vacated dream to the next.
He stretches and yawns
with all his teeth showing, obviously
something I admire.
Who watches me while I chase rabbits?
Who points and smiles?
Then whispers against my neck:
Turn over, stop shaking,
the small beast is already caught.

The Bird I'm Trying to Hold

Its wings beat against my hands, and I feel a corresponding
urge to exert a lot more pressure. Instead I release
a finger's worth of weight and stare out at the garden
I gave up on long before the first hard frost. I was practicing
how not to care. Let ripe tomatoes drop, basil go leggy
and bolt. But as per maxim the bird's come home to roost,
or I've hunted it down, or some anonymous third party's
intervened on behalf of whatever it is
that quick-crawls across my retina when I blink—a notion
not as bright as the red-wing blackbird's tell-tale epaulette
but just as exotic: compassion, loving, or trying to love,
what may have hurt you, what's apt to hurt you again.
As if to prove my point the bird twists her neck, tries to peck
at a knuckle, and I close my eyes, moving back and forth
between my mother's face as it is now, encased
in the mask of her illness, and my nursery school photo:
she standing behind where I'm posed in an oversized toy boat.
Our smiles are identical lines of straight, worried teeth.
Her waist cinched by her shirtdress, the bangs of her black hair
cut in an asymmetrical slant, no doubt by my father,
who even now believes he can do anything better.
She thinks so, too. And I'm not to disabuse either of them
on that point. Could but haven't. Which is the bird
I'm trying to hold. Which now and then stops struggling
long enough to ask if I'll ever guess the difference
between forgiveness and giving in.

How It Flew from Her

From her mouth. It gathered its small, soft body and leapt
forward, up and out. And then it was gone. She knew
because of the dark hollow in her chest, like the place a woodpecker
    makes,
keeps making, until it's emptied the wood of food
and moved on. She didn't try to stop it, because she didn't know
what it was; what came from her mouth
looked like a white moth, the kind that eats wool, so she clapped
    her hands,
chased it to the window, pulled the shade down
and pretended that was that. It's surprising it stayed
as long as it did, because most of all, she made it wait. She made
    it wait
while she beat a dead horse, hit the nail on the head, drove her
    point home,
split hairs, threw fat on the fire, killed birds with a stone.
Naturally, it grew tired of waiting,
tried to tell her, made a few practice runs, beat its wings;
she could feel it, don't tell me she couldn't, she could hear
the wings beat. She still feels it, like when you lose an arm or leg
and it aches but there's nothing there
to ache. That's how hollow she feels. She talks a lot, laughs
with her mouth open wide. Not everyone knows why,
but I do: she's making a place for it to come back to.

AMY DRYANSKY earned an M.F.A. in Poetry from Vermont College and a B.F.A from Syracuse University, where she studied painting, art history and aesthetics. She has been awarded residencies at the MacDowell Colony, Vermont Studio Center and Villa Montalvo, and a scholarship to the Bread Loaf Writers Conference. Born in Cleveland, she's lived in Amsterdam, London and upstate New York. She currently lives in western Massachusetts, where she leads writing workshops for women and girls, and works as a consultant to nonprofit arts organizations.

Recent Titles from Alice James Books

ALICE JAMES BOOKS has been publishing books since 1973. One of the few presses in the country that is run collectively, the cooperative selects manuscripts for publication through annual competitions. New authors become active members of the cooperative, participating in the editorial decisions of the press. The press, which places emphasis on publishing women poets, was named for Alice James, sister of William and Henry, whose gift for writing was ignored and whose fine journal did not appear until after her death.

How I Got Lost So Close to Home

This book was supported by a grant from
The Greenwall Fund of *The Academy of American Poets*